Matriarch: The Tina Knowles Memoir

The Untold Story of Strength, Style, and the Woman Behind the Legacy

C.J. Ellington

Copyright © 2025 by C.J. Ellington

Matriarch: The Tina Knowles Memoir

All rights reserved. No part of this publication may be reproduced, distributed, or transmitted in any form or by any means—electronic, mechanical, photocopying, recording, or otherwise—without the prior written permission of the author, except in the case of brief quotations used in critical reviews and articles.

This is a work of non-fiction. While every effort has been made to ensure the accuracy of the information presented, the author disclaims liability for any errors or omissions. The views and opinions expressed herein are those of the author and do not necessarily reflect the official policy or position of any related individual or entity.

Disclaimer

This book is intended for informational and inspirational purposes only. *Matriarch: The Tina Knowles Memoir* is an independent and original interpretation of the life, legacy, and influence of Tina Knowles, based on publicly available information, interviews, media coverage, and cultural impact. It is **not authorized, endorsed, or affiliated** with Tina Knowles, her family, or any associated entities.

While every effort has been made to ensure the accuracy and integrity of the content, the author does not claim to represent the personal views, private experiences, or direct words of Tina Knowles unless explicitly stated and sourced. Any resemblance to private conversations or unpublished material is purely coincidental or based on creative interpretation.

Readers are encouraged to explore official sources and verified interviews for additional context and information. The author and publisher disclaim any liability for inaccuracies, interpretations, or the use or misuse of the material presented herein.

Table of Contents

Introduction: Becoming the Matriarch

1. **Roots in Galveston**
   The early years, family background, and the shaping of a strong Black woman.

2. **A Dreamer with a Needle**
   How Tina discovered her love for beauty, fashion, and creating with her hands.

3. **Love, Loss & Reinvention**
   Marriage, motherhood, and the strength to rise from personal heartbreak.

4. **Raising Queens**
   The wisdom and intentional parenting behind Beyoncé and Solange's greatness.

5. **The House That Tina Built**
   Behind the scenes of Destiny's Child, costumes, branding, and motherly guidance.

6. **Style & Power**
   From salon chairs to couture — the evolution of Tina Knowles as a fashion icon.

7. **Second Chances, Timeless Love**
   Finding love again with Richard Lawson and

the beauty of healing.

8. **Mama Knows Best**
   Her philosophy on womanhood, family, culture, and generational strength.

9. **Philanthropy & Purpose**
   Tina's quiet empire of impact — from community to global influence.

10. **Legacy in Motion**
    The matriarchal mindset: how Tina shaped a lineage of power, purpose, and poise.

Epilogue: The Matriarch's Message to the World
About the Author

Introduction:
Becoming the Matriarch

Before the world knew her as Beyoncé and Solange's mother, before the spotlight found her in fashion houses, red carpets, and Grammy stages—Tina Knowles was a woman carving a path through quiet strength, deep faith, and creative brilliance. She was the backbone before the brand. The voice of reason in the chaos of fame. The steady hand that molded more than just garments—she shaped futures.

To understand Tina Knowles is to look beyond her last name and even beyond her maternal identity. It is to recognize the legacy of matriarchy not just in bloodline, but in *blueprint*. The word "matriarch" often conjures the image of an elder woman presiding over a large family—strong, wise, unshakable. Tina fits this definition, but she also transcends it. Her matriarchy is active, not passive. Strategic, not just emotional. It is stylish, not only spiritual. She has mothered stars, yes—but also movements, ideas, businesses, and communities.

Born Celestine Ann Beyincé in Galveston, Texas, Tina Knowles was raised in a home where pride, culture, and discipline were as present as prayer and hard work. Her Creole roots trace back to generations of resilience. The strength she now radiates was passed down through women who knew struggle intimately but never wore it as a chain. These were women who knew how to hold their heads high while building empires out of nothing. Tina learned early on that to be a woman—especially a Black woman in America—meant knowing how to stitch grace into survival.

Her life would go on to be defined by reinvention. From hairstylist to fashion designer, from wife to single mother, from the shadows of the stage to commanding one of her own—Tina's story is not one of privilege, but of persistent reinvention. She made mistakes. She made magic. She made masterpieces of moments most would have crumbled under. And through it all, she mothered the world's biggest stars with the same authenticity with which she ran a Houston salon.

But what does it really mean to "become" the matriarch?

It means stepping into leadership when life doesn't give you the luxury to wait. It means showing up strong even when you feel weak. It means protecting your children's dreams as fiercely as your own. For Tina Knowles, it meant daring to push her daughters toward excellence, even when the world didn't understand their greatness. It meant managing tours while designing stage outfits late into the night. It meant staying rooted when fame tried to pull her family in a hundred directions.

More than just "Beyoncé's mom," Tina has earned her place as a cultural matriarch. She has modeled a new type of mothering for a generation: one that is firm, visionary, stylish, and unapologetically Black. She is proof that you don't have to disappear behind your children's shine—you can reflect it, direct it, and still glow in your own right.

Matriarch: The Tina Knowles Memoir is not just a recounting of moments—it's an honoring of the mindset behind the woman. It is a deep dive into how love, faith, creativity, and inner fortitude can build legacies that outlive us. It explores how Tina's life—both public and private—laid the foundation for two global superstars, yes, but also for a deeper conversation on motherhood, womanhood, and the power of intention.

This book is for anyone who has ever stood behind the scenes, holding everything together. For the mother, the sister, the dreamer, the artist, the believer. For those who know what it is to sacrifice, to pray, to stitch strength into silence. For those becoming matriarchs in their own right.

Tina Knowles didn't just raise icons. She became one.

Chapter One

Roots in Galveston

The Early Years, Family Background, and the Shaping of a Strong Black Woman

Before Tina Knowles became a symbol of elegance, vision, and matriarchal strength, she was a young girl growing up in Galveston, Texas—a small island city resting quietly on the Gulf Coast, where the sea met southern soil and stories were passed down like heirlooms. In Galveston, time moved slower, the sun hung lower, and the air was thick with both humidity and history.

Tina was born **Celestine Ann Beyincé** on **January 4, 1954**, the youngest of seven children in a proud Creole family that deeply valued faith, discipline, and cultural heritage. Her family name—*Beyincé*, pronounced "bay-EN-say"—was itself a relic of a past tied to both African and French ancestry, a bridge between worlds and a symbol of survival. It would later become the root of one of the most recognizable names in global music: Beyoncé. But long before that transformation, it signified identity, legacy, and pride.

Her father, **Lumis Albert Beyincé**, was a longshoreman—a hard-working man whose hands bore the story of generations. Her mother, **Agnez Deréon**, was a skilled seamstress who made clothes not just to cover bodies, but to express identity. It was Agnez who would pass down the gift of design and detail to her daughter, never knowing it would one day shape the global fashion of Destiny's Child and beyond.

The Beyincé household was rich—not in wealth, but in principles. Every child had chores. Every child had rules. And Tina, though the youngest, was never coddled. From the earliest days, she was taught to walk with grace, speak with confidence, and carry herself as a lady. Her mother instilled in her a sense of *class*, a word Tina would revisit often in life—not to mean elitism, but *excellence in conduct, appearance, and soul.*

Though Galveston was charming, it was also deeply marked by the realities of segregation and racial inequality. The 1950s and '60s were turbulent times for Black families in the South. The opportunities were slim, the expectations lower, and the glass ceilings almost invisible—but ever-present. Tina grew up in an environment where Black excellence was not a luxury; it was a requirement for survival. You had to *be twice as good to get half as far*, and Tina learned early to meet every challenge with poise and preparation.

School was both a social platform and a proving ground. Tina stood out—not only because of her beauty, which had an effortless elegance, but because of her eye for design and her sharp sense of individuality. While other girls wore store-bought dresses, Tina would sometimes show up in outfits crafted from leftover fabrics and her mother's imagination. She learned the language of thread and pattern long before it became her profession.

But childhood was not without its trials. Tragedy struck when her father passed away during her teenage years. The loss shook the family to its core. Tina, still so young, found herself grieving not only the absence of her father but the sudden shift in family dynamics. It was in this crucible of loss and responsibility that she began to discover her deeper strength. Without the safety net of a father figure, she grew up fast. She began working early, helping around the house, watching her older siblings navigate adult responsibilities with the kind of grace she would come to model.

And yet, through the hardship, there was always music, laughter, and faith. Sundays were sacred. Church was not just a religious space—it was community, identity, and performance. Tina sang in choirs, wore Sunday dresses stitched with love, and watched women express their pride in the way they dressed, prayed, and praised. The church gave her a stage to observe the intersection of style and spirit—where your shoes were polished and your soul on fire.

From her earliest memories, Tina saw the women around her—her mother, her sisters, her neighbors—

as pillars of power. They held families together, kept dignity intact, and dared to dream bigger even when the world offered little in return. They were unshakable, even when life tried to break them. This was the inheritance Tina received—not gold or land, but *grit, grace, and greatness*.

In Galveston, the seeds of Tina's character were sown. It was there she learned how to balance strength with softness, how to walk into a room with intention, how to find beauty in the details. The island was small, but her dreams were not. Even as a child, Tina knew she was meant to touch the world—but she would do so in her own time, in her own way, and with her family beside her.

This chapter of her life—the quiet one, the formative one—is rarely spoken of in headlines or interviews. Yet it is here, in the heart of Galveston, that the *Matriarch* was born.

Chapter Two

A Dreamer with a Needle

How Tina Discovered Her Love for Beauty, Fashion, and Creating with Her Hands

Some women inherit jewels. Others inherit legacies. Tina Knowles inherited a *needle*—and with it, the power to create beauty, command attention, and craft dreams into tangible reality.

In the Beyincé household, the hum of a sewing machine was a familiar sound. Tina's mother, Agnez Deréon, was not simply a seamstress; she was an artist in her own right. Agnez had a vision—a keen eye for detail, symmetry, and fabric—and she expressed it with every stitch she made. For her, sewing was more than a task; it was a language of love, dignity, and aspiration. And little Tina was fluent in it from an early age.

Tina's earliest memories of fashion were soaked in color and creativity. She would watch her mother transform scraps of fabric into elegance, simple dresses into statements. Whether it was hemming a skirt for a neighbor or crafting a Sunday outfit for one of her daughters, Agnez imbued each creation with pride and precision. Young Tina was fascinated. She'd sit close, observing how hands moved methodically, how ideas came alive beneath spools of thread and beads, and how fashion could be both function and fantasy.

But Tina was not content with just watching. Before long, she began experimenting. First with dolls—cutting, tying, taping scraps of cloth onto them, dreaming of bigger canvases. Then with herself, designing her own clothes or altering what she was given. There was a thrill in being different, in wearing something no one else had. Her peers noticed, and so did the women in her community. She wasn't just a pretty girl—she had *taste.* Even then, her style stood out: elegant, bold, and intentional.

The act of creation was her first form of independence. She didn't need permission to dream. With a needle in hand, Tina found her power—a power she would carry into motherhood, business, and branding in the decades to come. She saw beauty not as luxury, but as a birthright. Every Black girl deserved to feel regal, celebrated, and confident, no matter where she came from.

Outside the home, however, the world wasn't always so receptive to her dreams. Fashion, in the 1960s and '70s, wasn't a clear or easily attainable career path for a young Black woman from Texas. The industry was white-dominated, class-driven, and often dismissive of Black creativity unless it could be commodified or copied. But Tina didn't need permission to innovate.

She didn't wait for doors to open—she learned to make her own.

After high school, she took her natural eye for design and turned it into skill. She trained professionally as a cosmetologist and later studied fashion design. She was drawn to the connection between hair, makeup, and fashion—the full spectrum of beauty and presentation. There was something sacred about helping someone feel transformed. Whether it was through a fresh hairstyle or a custom gown, Tina understood what it meant to *see* someone, to amplify their essence rather than mask it.

She eventually began working in salons, and it wasn't long before she became a trusted stylist and beauty expert in Houston. People came not just for services, but for the experience of Tina Knowles—the way she made them feel, the confidence she instilled, the beauty she drew out. By the time she opened her own salon, *Headliners*, she was not just styling clients—she was shaping identities, cultivating community, and sowing the seeds for something far bigger.

Fashion was never superficial for Tina. It was personal, political, and profoundly spiritual. She knew that a well-cut dress could change a woman's posture. That a bold red lip could embolden the voice. That presentation wasn't vanity—it was power. Especially for Black women, whose image and worth were constantly challenged, fashion became a means of resistance. A celebration of heritage. A language of empowerment.

And so, Tina stitched her way into destiny. Every pleat, every rhinestone, every feathered hem carried intention. She didn't know then that she was laying the foundation for *House of Deréon*, or that her future daughters would walk stages in her designs. She just knew she had a gift. A passion. A dream. And she was ready to use her hands to build the life her heart saw.

Looking back, it's clear: Tina's love for fashion was not born from magazines or Parisian catwalks. It was born in a humble Texas home, fed by her mother's hands, shaped by her own imagination, and refined through years of hard work. She wasn't chasing trends—she was defining identity.

Before she was a matriarch, Tina Knowles was a dreamer with a needle. And through her artistry, she would go on to dress not only her daughters—but a generation.

Chapter Three

Love, Loss & Reinvention

Marriage, Motherhood, and the Strength to Rise from Personal Heartbreak

Love has a way of shaping us—sometimes as a balm, sometimes as a furnace. For Tina Knowles, love would be both: the cornerstone of her legacy and the crucible that tested the depths of her strength.

By the time Tina met Mathew Knowles, she had already cultivated a quiet fire within. She was successful in her own right—working as a stylist, running a salon, and building a life anchored in purpose. Mathew, on the other hand, was a sharp, charismatic corporate executive with big dreams. When they crossed paths, their chemistry was undeniable—two driven minds, equally ambitious, equally aware that they could build something greater *together*.

Their love blossomed quickly, but not recklessly. Tina was no stranger to the weight of commitment. She'd seen both the beauty and the burdens of marriage in her own family. But with Mathew, she saw not just a partner, but a co-architect of the life she envisioned—a life where family came first, where creativity was nurtured, and where Black excellence was not only pursued but expected.

Their union brought forth two daughters: Beyoncé and Solange. And with motherhood, Tina found her truest calling. She poured her heart into nurturing not only their talent, but their character. Her home became both a sanctuary and a stage. While Mathew managed the logistics of the dream, Tina kept the soul of it alive. She cooked, designed, rehearsed, braided hair, prayed, corrected, and celebrated—doing a million unseen acts that ultimately shaped global icons.

But in many ways, motherhood was Tina's *first* masterpiece. She raised her daughters to know their worth, to walk in rooms with grace and intelligence, to be both vulnerable and fierce. And she did it all while continuing to run her salon, design costumes, and hold her household together.

From the outside, the Knowles family appeared invincible—beautiful, talented, successful. But behind the scenes, as is often the case with love stories, fractures began to form.

Years of business entanglement, the relentless pace of fame, and personal betrayals began to wear on Tina's marriage. The cracks widened with time. Whispers became wounds. And the woman who had so often held everyone else up found herself slowly unraveling under the weight of secrets and sorrow.

When Tina discovered Mathew's infidelity—and later, the children he fathered outside of their marriage—her world shifted. She was forced to confront a painful truth: that the life she built so carefully, the marriage she protected so fiercely, had changed beyond repair.

Divorce is never easy. But for a woman who spent her life nurturing others, choosing herself was revolutionary. After thirty-one years of marriage, Tina filed for divorce—not in bitterness, but in brave clarity. She chose peace over pretense. Healing over hiding. It was a decision that required immense courage, and it marked the beginning of her *reinvention*.

In the aftermath, Tina didn't just survive—she *transformed*. She leaned into her own voice, her own passions, her own healing. For years, her identity had been wrapped in titles: wife, mother, manager, designer. But now she began reclaiming the woman beneath those roles. She traveled more. She reconnected with old friends. She laughed again. She learned that heartbreak doesn't destroy you—it *reveals* you.

And then, when she least expected it, love found her again.

Richard Lawson, an actor and long-time family friend, entered Tina's life not with fireworks but with steady warmth. Where her previous marriage had been built on shared dreams, this new relationship was built on shared healing. Richard saw Tina—not as a vessel for others' greatness—but as the magnificent woman she was in her own right. In him, Tina found companionship, deep understanding, and most importantly, *joy*.

They married in 2015 in an all-white yacht ceremony surrounded by family, and it wasn't just a wedding—it was a reclamation. Tina walked into her second act not as a broken woman, but as a *matriarch* fully in bloom.

Her story became a living testimony: that a woman can love deeply, break deeply, and still rise higher. That marriage, while sacred, is not the only measure of a woman's worth. That motherhood is a gift, not a sacrifice of self. And that loss can be the beginning of becoming.

Through love, Tina discovered devotion. Through loss, she discovered resilience. And through reinvention, she discovered herself—not just as a woman behind a powerful family, but as a powerful force on her own.

Chapter Four

Raising Queens

The Wisdom and Intentional Parenting Behind Beyoncé and Solange's Greatness

To raise a child is to plant a seed in the soil of your values and water it with your every word, choice, and example. But to raise *Queens*—young women who not only carry themselves with grace, confidence, and brilliance but transform entire generations—requires something deeper. It takes *intention*. It takes *discipline*. It takes a sacred kind of *love*. And Tina Knowles understood that from the very beginning.

When Beyoncé Giselle Knowles and Solange Piaget Knowles came into Tina's life, she knew she wasn't just raising daughters. She was shaping women who would one day take up space in a world not designed for their kind of magic—a world that often devalues Black girls, questions their brilliance, and attempts to dim their light.

But Tina was never going to allow that—not in her house.

From a young age, Beyoncé and Solange were immersed in an environment of high standards and deep affection. Tina ran a tight ship, but she filled it with warmth. She believed in both structure and freedom—setting expectations while allowing her daughters to find their own paths. Her parenting style was rooted in empowerment. She didn't just tell her girls they were beautiful or talented—she made them *believe* it through consistent affirmation, honest conversations, and an unshakable belief in their uniqueness.

Discipline with Love

Tina was never the passive parent. She set boundaries early. Manners, humility, work ethic, and respect for others were non-negotiables. Beyoncé and Solange were not allowed to act entitled. Chores were a part of life. Accountability was a family value. Tina knew that fame or fortune could not protect her daughters from life's challenges—but resilience, character, and discipline *could*.

She often tells the story of how she would make Beyoncé sweep hair at the salon, or how Solange was expected to participate in family responsibilities despite her creative temperament. Tina believed in teaching by doing—instilling the principle that no task is beneath you and that success is earned, not handed down.

Cultivating Identity

What's most remarkable about Tina's parenting is how she nurtured two powerhouses with distinct voices and identities. Beyoncé, the perfectionist and quiet storm, was a born leader—meticulous, focused, and intensely private. Solange, on the other hand, was a free spirit—

rebellious, outspoken, and experimental. Tina never tried to mold them into copies of each other. Instead, she honored their differences and provided each with space to grow into her own woman.

She encouraged Beyoncé's focus and discipline, but also reminded her to rest, to reflect, to remain humble. With Solange, she celebrated her creativity and passion, while guiding her through the growing pains of carving out an unconventional path.

Tina often acted as both buffer and bridge. When the world tried to pit them against each other, she reminded them that their bond as sisters—and as Black women—was sacred. She taught them not to compete, but to complete one another. That kind of wisdom would later become the invisible thread that connected their individual successes and collective strength.

Beauty Beyond the Mirror

As a hairdresser and designer, Tina had a unique platform to influence how her daughters viewed beauty. But she never allowed it to be skin-deep. Yes, she made sure they looked the part—well-groomed, fashionable, poised—but she constantly emphasized that beauty without substance was a fleeting thing.

She would often say, "Pretty is as pretty does." Her daughters heard that phrase so often it became part of their inner voice. For Tina, beauty was not just about appearance—it was about kindness, confidence, and how you treated people when no one was watching.

She also knew the importance of seeing themselves reflected in their surroundings. Tina deliberately surrounded her daughters with images, stories, and role models that affirmed their Blackness and brilliance. She filled their bookshelves and walls with stories of Black excellence, and reminded them that their hair, skin, and culture were not burdens—but *crowns*.

Empowering with Purpose

Tina also taught her daughters to understand their platform as more than performance. She instilled in them a deep sense of responsibility—to speak up, to give back, to use their influence for good. That sense of purpose would go on to define both Beyoncé's and Solange's careers—not just as artists, but as activists and advocates for justice, womanhood, and the Black experience.

She reminded them of their roots in Houston. She encouraged them to know their grandparents' stories, to give thanks to the ancestors who paved the way. Tina made sure that fame never disconnected them from *who* they were and *whose* they were.

The Village

Tina also knew she wasn't doing it alone. She believed in the power of a village. Her own parents, her siblings, and later her extended family—Kelly Rowland, Michelle Williams, close friends—all played roles in helping shape her daughters. She cultivated an ecosystem of support, love, and accountability. She raised her girls to be loyal to their tribe and to understand the value of deep, authentic relationships.

Letting Go, Holding On

Perhaps the most bittersweet aspect of raising powerful children is knowing when to let go. Tina learned that lesson in her own time. As her daughters grew into women, wives, and mothers themselves, she transitioned from caretaker to confidante. From authority to advisor. It's a role she embraced with grace—remaining present but not controlling, involved but never intrusive.

Her greatest pride is not just in what her daughters have achieved—but in *who* they've become. Women of integrity. Women who use their voice. Women who lift others.

The Matriarch's Legacy

Tina Knowles didn't raise global icons by accident. She did it with a blueprint: love, discipline, authenticity, faith, and wisdom. Her daughters didn't just inherit talent—they inherited vision. They inherited grit. They inherited the quiet strength of a mother who never stopped believing that her girls could change the world.

And they did.

Because she did.

Chapter Five

The House That Tina Built

Behind the Scenes of Destiny's Child — Costumes, Branding, and Motherly Guidance

Long before the world knew them as Destiny's Child—the chart-topping, barrier-breaking, Grammy-winning powerhouse group—there was another force working just as tirelessly behind the scenes. Not a manager, not a music producer, but a mother. A matriarch. A visionary. Her name was Tina Knowles.

While the music industry spotlight was reserved for young performers, it was often the parents who toiled in the shadows, investing time, money, and love to nurture their children's dreams. Tina Knowles was no exception. But what set her apart was not just the fact that she supported her daughter's journey—it was how she *built* a world around that journey. A world that balanced artistry with protection, creativity with strategy, and glamour with grit.

This chapter is the story of how Tina Knowles created not only the costumes, but the *culture* of Destiny's Child—thread by thread, stage by stage.

A Family Business from Day One

When Beyoncé showed early signs of talent and drive, Tina and her then-husband Mathew Knowles became her biggest champions. But they weren't simply cheerleaders—they became co-architects of her career. As Destiny's Child began to take shape, with local performances, talent shows, and small tours, the Knowles household transformed into a headquarters for ambition.

Tina, already an accomplished hair stylist and fashion designer in Houston, knew that presentation was just as vital as performance. She understood instinctively what the world would later learn: in entertainment, *branding* matters. And long before Destiny's Child became a brand, Tina was building its foundation with her bare hands.

The Sewing Machine & the Spotlight

Money was tight in those early days. Hiring professional stylists and designers was not an option. So, Tina turned their modest means into a canvas for innovation. With her sewing machine, fabric from local stores, and an eye for symmetry, she began creating custom stage outfits for the girls. These weren't just clothes—they were *statements*. Tina crafted looks that elevated her daughter and her bandmates from local performers to stars-in-the-making.

Matching outfits. Coordinated themes. Flashy, but tasteful. Bold, but age-appropriate. Tina's designs told a story—a story of unity, sisterhood, and rising Black excellence. Whether it was camouflage cargo for "Survivor," bedazzled denim for "Bootylicious," or metallic glam for award shows, Tina's fashion sense gave the group a consistent identity.

But it wasn't just about aesthetics. Each stitch carried *purpose*. She made the girls feel confident and fierce. She made them stand out. She made them believe they belonged on the biggest stages in the world, even when those stages seemed out of reach.

Branding Before It Was Trendy

Today, branding is a buzzword tossed around by artists, marketers, and influencers alike. But Tina was already doing it intuitively in the late '90s. She helped define the look and feel of Destiny's Child as much as the music itself did. Tina knew that visual identity could be a secret weapon—a way to etch the group into public memory.

From hairstyles and accessories to music video aesthetics and red carpet glam, Tina curated the group's public image with the same care a designer builds a fashion house. She made sure each look aligned with the message of the moment. More than outfits, she created *uniforms* of empowerment.

And she did it with love, not ego. She wasn't interested in recognition. She was interested in *impact*.

A Mother Among Daughters

As Destiny's Child evolved, fame intensified. The pressure grew. The spotlight became more blinding. And while Mathew Knowles managed the business, it was Tina who managed the emotional and spiritual well-being of the group. The girls weren't just performers—many were teenagers, far from home, trying to make sense of stardom.

Tina became the nurturer. The confidante. The safe space. She traveled with the group, handled wardrobe changes, listened when they cried, and reminded them to stay grounded. She knew when to push and when to pause. She encouraged professionalism, but never at the cost of authenticity.

Beyoncé has often credited her mother as a stabilizing force—not just for her, but for everyone around her. Kelly Rowland has spoken publicly about how Tina took her in as a daughter, offering the same structure and unconditional love. Michelle Williams, too, felt Tina's warmth. It wasn't just Tina's designs that held the group together—it was her heart.

Fame, Fire, and Female Power

As Destiny's Child rose to global fame, their music evolved into anthems of empowerment: *Independent Women*, *Survivor*, *Say My Name*. These weren't just catchy tunes—they were cultural declarations. And behind those declarations was a woman who had taught her daughters—and all the girls under her wing—what strength looked like.

Tina's influence wasn't limited to fabric and fashion. It was foundational to the values the group projected. She reminded them of who they were, what they stood for, and what they represented: Black girls from the South rewriting history, without apology.

She shielded them from exploitation. She insisted on self-respect. She taught them to say "no" when necessary, to speak up when it mattered, and to know their worth even when others tried to diminish it.

The Birth of House of Deréon

Tina's dedication to fashion and her daughters' image eventually led to something more official—the birth of **House of Deréon**, a fashion label co-founded by Tina and Beyoncé. Named after Tina's own mother, Agnèz Deréon, a skilled seamstress in her own right, the brand honored a legacy of Black women who created beauty through thread and vision.

House of Deréon was more than a clothing line—it was a cultural homage. Tina infused it with heritage, elegance, and edge. It was a declaration that style and story could coexist, that Black excellence could wear couture and history at the same time.

Though House of Deréon was eventually phased out, its significance remained: Tina had not only dressed icons—she had become one herself.

Legacy in Every Stitch

Today, Tina Knowles is celebrated not just as the mother of Beyoncé and Solange, but as a pioneering creative in her own right. Her role in Destiny's Child was never secondary. She *built* the house—literally and metaphorically—that the girls could thrive in.

She taught them that greatness starts with preparation. That looking the part helps *becoming* the part. That showing up with excellence is a form of rebellion in a world that expects less of you.

The house that Tina built didn't have walls. It had values. It didn't need blueprints. It had belief. And while the members of Destiny's Child grew up and grew into new phases of life, Tina's fingerprints remained on everything they touched.

Because she wasn't just sewing costumes.

She was sewing *destiny*.

Chapter Six

Style & Power

From Salon Chairs to Couture — The Evolution of Tina Knowles as a Fashion Icon

Tina Knowles did not just *witness* style—she *defined* it. Long before the red carpets, luxury labels, and fashion spreads, her legacy was already being woven through the threads of Houston's working-class neighborhoods. Her story is not one of overnight success but of slow, intentional transformation—an evolution that began behind salon chairs and eventually commanded the front row of fashion shows.

This chapter is the powerful journey of how Tina Knowles transcended the expectations of her environment, culture, and era to become a quiet force in the fashion world—a matriarch of beauty and expression whose influence cannot be overstated.

The Beauty Shop as a Cultural Sanctuary

Tina's entrance into the world of style was not through runways or design schools—it was through the rhythmic buzz of clippers, the aroma of hair oils, and the sacred conversations between women in the salon.

Her beauty salon in Houston was more than a business; it was a cultural sanctuary.

There, women from all walks of life came not just to get their hair done, but to be seen, heard, and healed. Tina had an instinct for what made a woman feel beautiful—not only on the outside, but in her spirit. Her sense of aesthetic was never just cosmetic. It was spiritual. Empowering. A crown of dignity in a world that often tried to strip Black women of their shine.

As she worked her hands through strands of hair, she was also sculpting her future in fashion. The salon was her training ground. Her lab. It taught her that every woman had a story—and fashion, like hair, was a way to *tell it*.

Sewing for the Soul

Parallel to her work in beauty, Tina continued to feed her passion for fashion. Inspired by her mother, Agnèz Deréon, who had been a gifted seamstress, Tina began designing and sewing clothing for her daughters, friends, and eventually the emerging music group that would become Destiny's Child.

Her style merged Southern glam with streetwise flair. It was bold, expressive, unapologetically Black. Tina didn't just follow trends—she *created* them. She understood that clothes could be armor, celebration, rebellion, and storytelling—all at once.

Even before major designers would offer their creations to Beyoncé and Solange, it was Tina's handiwork that graced album covers, tour stages, and red carpets. She had a unique ability to blend accessibility with elegance, affordability with sophistication.

And she made it all look effortless.

Turning Heads in Couture

Eventually, as her daughters gained global fame, Tina's style journey expanded to new heights. She was no longer simply the behind-the-scenes stylist; she had become a fashion icon in her own right. Designers began to take note of her eye for detail, her sharp instincts, and her timeless glamor.

What made Tina stand out was her refusal to be boxed in. She didn't conform to fashion's rigid definitions of age, color, or silhouette. Instead, she *redefined* them. Her looks radiated class, strength, and sensuality. She was never afraid to show off her curves, wear bright colors, or embrace dramatic accessories. Her fashion sense was a message: Black women of *any* age can be vibrant, daring, and absolutely unforgettable.

In interviews and on social media, fans began to notice her elegance—and emulate it. Tina became the blueprint for mature style: poised but playful, refined yet relevant.

The Birth of House of Deréon

With Beyoncé as both muse and partner, Tina co-founded *House of Deréon*, a fashion line named in honor of her mother. This was a full-circle moment. Three generations of Black women, each with needle and thread in their hands, now had a label that stood for their legacy.

House of Deréon was more than fashion—it was *culture*. The line pulled from Creole roots, Southern beauty, and urban edge. It was modern, feminine, and rooted in heritage. While the brand eventually closed, its influence endured. It paved the way for other celebrity fashion lines and showed that a Black woman-led brand could succeed on its own terms.

Tina had proven that fashion wasn't just for Paris ateliers—it was for Houston kitchens, Black hair salons, and tour buses. And it could rise all the way to runways.

Style as a Platform for Purpose

As Tina's public profile grew, she began using her fashion influence to support causes she believed in—especially women's empowerment. Whether she was attending galas, walking with pride at Black Lives Matter protests in stylish attire, or supporting young designers and artists, she wore her values as clearly as she wore her clothes.

She also became a role model for aging gracefully and powerfully. In an industry obsessed with youth, Tina showed that style deepens with time. Her silver-streaked hair, regal poise, and radiant confidence inspired countless women to reclaim their power and visibility.

Her Instagram presence further cemented this. Posts of her dancing, creating, and giving fashion tips—often humorously—turned her into a beloved icon for new generations. Through style, she communicated joy, resilience, and authenticity.

A Fashion Matriarch

Today, Tina Knowles is more than Beyoncé's mom or Destiny's Child's stylist—she is a *fashion matriarch*. She represents the journey of Black women who used fashion as a means of self-expression, survival, and storytelling. Her name belongs alongside those who revolutionized how we see style—not just on bodies, but in *hearts*.

She has reminded us that the most powerful outfit is confidence. That real beauty is about how you carry pain, purpose, and passion with poise. That it's not about labels—it's about *legacy*.

Tina didn't just design dresses.

She designed *generations*.

Chapter Seven

Second Chances, Timeless Love

Finding love again with Richard Lawson and the beauty of healing

By the time Tina Knowles met Richard Lawson again—as more than a friend, more than a familiar face in passing—she had already lived an entire lifetime. She had been a daughter, a wife, a mother, a fashion designer, a businesswoman, and the anchor of one of the most influential families in entertainment. She had weathered heartbreak, held the hands of her daughters through every storm, and redefined herself after divorce.

But there is a quiet, sacred power in choosing to *begin again*. To open the heart once more. And in doing so, Tina discovered that love, in its purest form, doesn't arrive only once—it often comes *when you are finally ready to receive it*.

This is the chapter where the matriarch lets down her guard and invites love to enter through a different door—not through youthful passion, but through soulful connection. It is a love story not only about romance, but about healing, grace, and the courage to believe in joy again.

The End of One Chapter

Tina's marriage to Mathew Knowles was not only a romantic partnership; it was a professional empire. Together, they built the careers of their daughters and managed Destiny's Child at the height of its global success. But behind the scenes, Tina began to feel the erosion of trust and intimacy—an unraveling that would eventually lead to their separation in 2009 and divorce in 2011.

That season was heavy with disappointment. Divorce is never just about the end of a relationship—it's about the shifting of dreams, identity, and stability. For someone like Tina, who had poured herself into her family, the rupture of her marriage felt like both a personal and public loss.

But instead of closing in, Tina chose to grow *outward*. She deepened her spiritual practice, focused on her health, embraced therapy, and leaned into her community. Her daughters, who had always leaned on her, now wrapped her in their strength.

The heartbreak didn't defeat her. It *refined* her.

Richard: A Love Reborn

Tina had known Richard Lawson for decades. A respected actor with a rich legacy in television and film, he had long been part of her extended circle. But they had never crossed the threshold into romance—until the timing aligned, and both of them were finally free, emotionally and spiritually, to see each other fully.

Their love story didn't start with fireworks—it started with friendship, familiarity, and the comfort of shared history. And then it bloomed into something deeper.

Richard brought a calmness to Tina's life. He was attentive, thoughtful, and steady. Where others saw Tina as Beyoncé and Solange's mother or the powerful businesswoman behind the scenes, Richard saw *Tina*. The woman. The artist. The soul.

Their relationship wasn't rushed. It was intentional. They talked for hours, laughed about the past, dreamed about the future. He supported her ambitions, admired her creativity, and honored her resilience. It was the kind of love that comes not from needing someone to complete you—but from *already being whole*, and finding someone who recognizes that wholeness.

The Wedding on a Yacht

On April 12, 2015, at the age of 61, Tina Knowles became Tina Knowles-Lawson. Their wedding took place on a yacht in Newport Beach, California, surrounded by family and close friends—including Beyoncé, Solange, Blue Ivy, and Jay-Z.

She wore a flowing white gown and a crown of fresh flowers. The ocean stretched endlessly behind them, a metaphor for the vast new chapter that lay ahead. It was more than a wedding—it was a declaration: *You can start over. You can love again. And you can do it on your own terms.*

Her daughters beamed with pride. They had watched their mother suffer in silence, pick herself up, and now walk into a love that *chose her back*.

Healing Through Partnership

Richard became more than a husband—he became Tina's partner in philanthropy, creativity, and purpose. Together, they hosted art events, supported youth empowerment initiatives, and poured into the causes they cared about.

With Richard, Tina rediscovered her voice in a new way. She allowed herself to be nurtured. To be soft. To let someone else lead sometimes. She learned that vulnerability is not weakness—it is *a bridge to intimacy*.

She has spoken often about how surprised she was by the joy she felt in this chapter of life. Many women are taught that romance is for the young, that after 50, you fade into the background. Tina proved the opposite. She *glowed*—inside and out.

Their love was not perfect—but it was sacred. It was built on mutual respect, emotional intelligence, and a deep reverence for second chances.

Legacy of Love

In loving again, Tina set a new standard—not just for her daughters, but for every woman watching. She taught us that the end of one story doesn't mean the end of *your* story. That love is not about age—it's about alignment. That healing is not just internal—it can also happen in the presence of someone who sees you clearly and honors your scars.

Her relationship with Richard is not just about romance; it is a living testament that a woman can reinvent herself *as many times as necessary*. And each reinvention can be more powerful than the last.

Tina Knowles-Lawson stands as a matriarch not just because of what she built for others—but because she dared to rebuild *herself*.

Chapter Eight

Mama Knows Best

Her philosophy on womanhood, family, culture, and generational strength

To the world, Tina Knowles-Lawson is many things: designer, entrepreneur, mother of megastars, and icon in her own right. But to those closest to her—and to the millions who have watched her from afar—she is one thing above all else: **Mama**.

Not just *a* mother, but *the* mother. The nurturing force. The fire behind the throne. The guiding hand in the lives of Beyoncé and Solange—and by extension, in the evolution of Black womanhood on the world stage. But Tina's role as "Mama" is not limited to her biological children. It's a title she wears in the culture, in her community, and in her own soul. It is the identity through which she leads, nurtures, protects, and teaches.

And make no mistake—**Mama knows best**.

The Power of a Woman's Voice

From a young age, Tina was taught the value of a woman's voice. Raised in Galveston, Texas, she watched her mother Celestine Ann Beyincé serve her family with grace and grit. She wasn't just a homemaker—she was an example of *Black excellence in action*, even in the face of racism, economic struggle, and societal limitations.

Tina learned early that womanhood wasn't about submission—it was about *strength, strategy, and softness interwoven*. Her philosophy grew from that foundation: that a woman should be powerful but never lose her compassion, beautiful but never defined by appearance, assertive but never without wisdom.

Tina would go on to pour this into every corner of her life. Whether she was managing a salon, building a fashion line, or preparing her daughters for the spotlight, she rooted every action in the belief that **a woman's intuition, if respected, is an unshakable compass**.

Family is the First Empire

For Tina, family has always been sacred. She didn't just raise her children—she *built a dynasty* by instilling purpose, discipline, humility, and pride in one's roots.

Tina wasn't interested in raising famous daughters. She was determined to raise *good women*. Women who were educated, grounded, spiritually aware, and deeply connected to their ancestry and community.

Her home was not just a house—it was a *school of life*. A place where creative expression was encouraged, chores taught responsibility, and dinner table conversations turned into masterclasses on Black history, womanhood, and the world.

She created a culture of intentional parenting: listening without judgment, correcting with love, and leading by example. That's why Beyoncé and Solange, despite their fame, remain tethered to their roots. Because Tina didn't just birth them—she *formed* them.

Culture Keeper

Tina Knowles-Lawson has long been a custodian of Black culture—through fashion, storytelling, and the intentional celebration of heritage.

She taught her daughters to embrace their African-American identity proudly, to understand their lineage, and to use their platforms to uplift their people. When Destiny's Child took the stage in Ankara prints or Solange curated visuals filled with ancestral symbolism, that wasn't just artistic flair—it was **Mama's influence**, embedded deep in their creative DNA.

Tina believed that representation wasn't a trend; it was a duty. Whether in clothing design, media presence, or community engagement, she championed the elegance, creativity, and resilience of Black women.

She became a cultural architect behind the scenes, ensuring that every thread, every lyric, every choice paid homage to a broader Black narrative. Her commitment turned her family into *ambassadors of culture*.

Womanhood Reimagined

To Tina, being a woman has never been about fitting into boxes—it's been about *redesigning the blueprint*.

She redefined what it meant to be a mother in the public eye—balancing ambition with caretaking, business with softness, legacy with flexibility. She gave herself permission to grow, evolve, and pursue her dreams even after raising children.

She has also spoken openly about aging with grace and confidence, rejecting the idea that a woman's worth diminishes with time. Instead, she models the truth that *maturity is a superpower*, and that wisdom gives a woman her fiercest edge.

Tina's beauty philosophy is simple: radiance begins within. And her life proves it.

Generational Strength

Tina didn't just pass down talents—she passed down *tools*. Tools for navigating life, business, heartbreak, success, and identity.

She believes that generational wealth isn't just financial—it's **emotional intelligence, cultural memory, and character**. That's why, through her charity work, mentorship, and philanthropy, she has extended her influence beyond her immediate family to shape a new generation of creatives, dreamers, and leaders.

In her daughters' strength, you see Tina's endurance. In their activism, her values. In their elegance, her blueprint.

She is a bridge between generations. Between the wisdom of her ancestors and the innovation of her descendants. A living example of what happens when a woman builds not just a family, but a **foundation**.

Mama Knows Best, Because Mama *Lived* It

Tina Knowles-Lawson's philosophy is not written in theory—it's forged in fire. She has walked through disappointment, disillusionment, and pressure, and emerged more grounded than ever. Her words carry weight because they come with *receipts*—of loyalty, love, and labor.

She reminds us that being a matriarch doesn't mean being perfect—it means being *present*. It means showing up with wisdom, leading with empathy, and never forgetting that the world changes when a woman understands her power.

Mama knows best—not because she's always had the answers, but because she's lived the questions, honored the journey, and passed the torch.

And the world is brighter for it.

Chapter Nine

Philanthropy & Purpose

Tina's Quiet Empire of Impact — From Community to Global Influence

There are empires built of gold, and there are empires built of *good*. Tina Knowles-Lawson has crafted both. While her more public legacy is anchored in beauty, fashion, and motherhood to music royalty, her most enduring impact may well be in the lives she's touched quietly—away from the lights and applause.

Behind every iconic costume, behind the global tours, and red carpets, lies the soul of a woman driven not by vanity or validation, but by *purpose*. To know Tina is to know her heart for people—especially *her people*. Her philanthropy isn't performative. It's personal. It's generational. And it is intentional.

Roots of Purpose: Giving Begins at Home

Growing up in Galveston, Texas, Tina watched her parents model compassion in action. Her mother was known for feeding neighbors, taking in children who weren't hers, and offering dignity to the underserved. That kind of giving wasn't celebrated—it was expected.

Tina internalized this truth early: **to whom much is given, much is required**.

Long before the world knew her name, Tina was already helping, guiding, supporting. Whether it was mentoring young hairstylists in her salon or helping neighbors find work, she understood that influence, no matter how small, could shift someone's entire life.

That local spirit of giving never left her. Even as her reach expanded globally, her philanthropy remained *intimately human*.

The Knowles-Rowland Center: Planting Seeds

In 2002, Tina joined forces with daughter Beyoncé and close family friend Kelly Rowland to establish the **Knowles-Rowland Center for Youth** in Houston, Texas. This wasn't just a gesture—it was *a statement*.

The center offers housing, counseling, and resources to disadvantaged young people in their community. It stands as a monument to Tina's belief in second chances and building from the ground up. Her approach was never about throwing money at problems—it was about *creating solutions*, rooted in dignity and empowerment.

What made the center unique was Tina's *active involvement*. She wasn't just a name on the board; she engaged directly, visited regularly, and ensured that the young people felt seen—not saved, but *supported*.

Where Art Meets Action: WACO Theater Center

One of Tina's most passionate and visible endeavors is the **WACO Theater Center**, co-founded with her husband, actor Richard Lawson. WACO—which stands for *Where Art Can Occur*—was born from their shared mission to empower artists of color and provide a creative sanctuary for underrepresented voices.

Through WACO, Tina helps produce art that challenges, educates, and uplifts. The center hosts workshops, youth mentorship programs, and live performances. Its annual **Wearable Art Gala**, which Tina curates with her signature flair, raises funds to support the organization's programs while celebrating Black excellence in art, design, and performance.

WACO isn't just a theater—it's a cultural movement. It's Tina's declaration that art isn't a luxury for the elite, but a *lifeline for the silenced*. Through this platform, she is nurturing the next generation of changemakers, just as she nurtured her daughters.

Philanthropy as Legacy: Giving Beyond the Spotlight

Tina's philanthropic touch extends far beyond brick-and-mortar institutions. She has quietly supported a variety of causes: domestic violence shelters, education initiatives, disaster relief efforts, women's empowerment organizations, and mentorship programs.

What's remarkable is her consistency. Long before hashtags and headlines, Tina was on the ground, writing checks, showing up, and using her access to open doors for others. She has always preferred *impact over impression*.

Even her fashion work has had philanthropic ripples—employing women in need, collaborating with local designers, and ensuring that her projects create opportunities in overlooked spaces.

Her humility in this work is part of what makes it so powerful. Tina rarely seeks credit; instead, she sees giving as *a moral contract*, a sacred responsibility tied to her faith and her heritage.

Global Ripple Effect

Though Tina's heart beats for her community, her influence spans continents. Through Beyoncé's charitable arm, **BeyGOOD**, and Solange's cultural projects, Tina's philanthropic values have gone global.

Disaster relief in Haiti. Scholarships for students across Africa. Women's health initiatives. Legal aid for unjustly incarcerated individuals. These are just some of the global causes indirectly powered by Tina's influence and vision.

She didn't just teach her daughters to give—she taught them *how to give wisely, boldly, and consistently*. And as they carry the torch into massive global platforms, Tina's legacy is etched in every life they touch.

The Heart of It All: Why Tina Gives

For Tina, philanthropy isn't about wealth—it's about **worth**. She sees people not for what they have, but for who they are and *who they can become*. Her core belief is that everyone deserves access, dignity, and the chance to thrive.

Giving, to her, is an act of *justice*. A form of *love*. A tool of *liberation*.

She often says that legacy isn't just what you build, but *who you help build themselves*. That is the essence of Tina Knowles-Lawson's quiet empire: a mosaic of lives uplifted, doors opened, voices amplified, and dreams given permission to fly.

Matriarch of the Movement

Tina's philanthropy mirrors the very essence of her matriarchal role. Just as she raised two powerful daughters, she has helped raise a generation of dreamers, creators, and believers.

She is not only the mother of Beyoncé and Solange. She is a mother to the movement—a *matriarch of modern giving*. Her work doesn't always make the headlines, but its echoes will be felt for generations.

Tina Knowles-Lawson reminds us that purpose is the heartbeat of legacy—and that **the most powerful empires are built in the service of others**.

Chapter Ten

Legacy in Motion

The Matriarchal Mindset: How Tina Shaped a Lineage of Power, Purpose, and Poise

Legacy is not only what you leave *behind*; it's what you leave *within* others. For Tina Knowles-Lawson, legacy is an active force—a living, breathing continuum of values, vision, and voice passed down from generation to generation. It is not confined to wealth or notoriety, but rooted in *how you love, how you lead, and how you lift others.*

From Galveston to global stages, Tina has moved through life with the quiet authority of a woman who knows her worth—and knows how to cultivate that worth in others. This chapter explores how she forged a matriarchal lineage marked by strength, intention, grace, and enduring cultural influence.

A Matriarch's Mindset

To be a matriarch is not merely to hold a title in the family hierarchy—it is to *become the emotional, spiritual, and moral anchor* of a tribe. Tina embodies this role with intentionality. Her leadership is not loud, but it is firm. Her decisions are laced with wisdom, and her instincts are led by love.

She sees beyond the present moment, nurturing not just her daughters' careers but their *souls*. She has always known that power without grounding is dangerous. So she raised grounded women. Poise without purpose is hollow. So she taught purpose. Fame without faith can be fleeting. So she instilled values that could weather any storm.

Tina did not just birth stars. She shaped *luminaries with lasting depth*.

Lineage of Leadership: Beyoncé and Solange

Tina's daughters are household names, but their success is not an accident. It is a reflection of the foundation they were built upon—a foundation of hard work, cultural pride, independence, and self-worth.

Beyoncé, often hailed as the greatest entertainer of her generation, carries her mother's discipline and strategic brilliance. Her work ethic, perfectionism, and quiet philanthropy all echo Tina's standards. Beyond the glitz, Beyoncé remains rooted in Black excellence, women's empowerment, and ownership—values she absorbed from watching her mother's relentless pursuit of greatness on her own terms.

Solange, an avant-garde creative force, channels her mother's soulful expression and fearless individuality. From her music to her visual art, Solange celebrates Black womanhood, southern culture, and healing—all pillars of Tina's worldview. Solange didn't conform to the industry's mold; she carved her own space, just as Tina had done decades earlier in her salon, studio, and life.

Together, Beyoncé and Solange represent *different expressions of the same truth*: that true power lies in authenticity, artistry, and ancestral alignment. Tina raised them to be queens—but *not of others' kingdoms*. She raised them to rule *their own*.

Cultural Stewardship: Guarding the Legacy

Tina's legacy extends far beyond her biological lineage. She has served as a cultural steward for Black womanhood, southern identity, and generational healing. Whether through her style influence, community work, or storytelling, she has preserved and promoted the richness of African-American heritage.

Her work reminds Black women that they can be *soft and strong, glamorous and grounded, bold and benevolent*—all at once. She redefined what it means to age with power, mother with purpose, and lead with love.

Every gala she curates, every young girl she mentors, every business she builds—it's all part of a wider ecosystem of elevation. Tina isn't just passing down stories—she's passing down standards.

Mothering the Culture

It's no coincidence that fans often refer to Tina as "Mama Tina." It's more than a nickname; it's a *collective recognition* of her nurturing spirit. Across social media, interviews, and appearances, Tina is seen giving affirmations, celebrating others' milestones, and offering sage wisdom. She shows up—not just for her daughters, but for the culture.

Her platform is not used for spectacle, but for *substance*. She mothers an entire generation—young creatives, Black girls finding their voice, women rediscovering their power. She models a womanhood that is rich in legacy and unapologetic in its strength.

Teaching the Next Matriarchs

Tina understands that legacy is not about what she controls, but what she *empowers*. She has always been a teacher—whether through example, conversation, or design. She teaches that beauty is deeper than skin. That success must be purposeful.

That healing is holy. And that your crown is only as powerful as the people you lift with it.

Her life is a curriculum. Her resilience is the textbook. Her love is the lesson plan.

As Beyoncé becomes a matriarch in her own right, and as Solange nurtures her own creative lineage, Tina's teachings ripple through time. They will guide future mothers, artists, leaders, and dreamers. Because when a matriarch like Tina plants seeds, she doesn't just grow daughters—*she grows dynasties.*

Legacy as a Living Flame

In the end, Tina Knowles-Lawson's legacy is not just her past—it's her *presence*. It's not just what she leaves *when she's gone*, but what she gives *while she's here*. Her legacy is motion. It is energy. It is the flicker in a young Black girl's eyes when she sees a woman like Tina and thinks, *"I can build that. I can be that."*

She is a matriarch not because of what she holds, but because of what she gives away—wisdom, courage, elegance, and truth.

And so her story continues—not in history books alone, but in every life touched by her grace.

Chapter 11

Epilogue: The Matriarch's Message to the World

+ Acknowledgments

The final word in any legacy story isn't just a conclusion—it's a *commission*. As Tina Knowles-Lawson reflects on the chapters of her life, from the modest neighborhoods of Galveston to international red carpets and philanthropic platforms, her message to the world is one of power, purpose, and generational grace.

She stands now not simply as a mother, a designer, or a cultural force—but as a *matriarch*. And from that sacred position, she sends forth a message not wrapped in vanity or status—but in *truth*.

To Women: Reclaim Your Narrative

Tina's message to women everywhere is simple, yet revolutionary: *Own your story. Rewrite it if you must. But never let anyone else hold the pen.*

She encourages every woman—whether in the salon, the boardroom, the classroom, or the kitchen—to lead with love, create from the soul, and believe that it is never too late to start again.

She is living proof that even in the midst of heartbreak, betrayal, or self-doubt, a woman can *reinvent herself without apology*. That beauty is not confined to youth, nor is success confined to men. And that being "soft" and "strong" are not opposites—they are *complements*.

To Mothers: You're Building Kingdoms

Her message to mothers is a reminder of their sacred assignment. Every lesson taught, every word spoken, every hug given or withheld becomes part of a child's inner world. Tina urges mothers to *parent with intention*, to plant seeds of excellence, creativity, faith, and truth.

She shares that greatness in children is not merely discovered—it is *nurtured*. Beyoncé and Solange were not born icons. They were raised by one.

But she also reminds mothers to take care of *themselves*. That martyrdom is not motherhood. That healing is a gift to your lineage. And that every mother deserves to evolve—even while she's raising others.

To Artists & Creators: Make Beauty That Matters

Tina's journey as a designer, stylist, and creative director has always been driven by one conviction: *Fashion is a form of storytelling.* Through fabric, form, and flair, she told stories about Black beauty, pride, and royalty. She showed the world that art can be commercial *and* cultural.

Her message to creators is this: *Don't just create to be seen. Create to be remembered.* Make art that empowers, that lifts, that challenges norms and redefines standards. And never underestimate the power of your gift—it may be the very tool God gave you to shift generations.

To the Black Community: We Are the Legacy

For Tina, Blackness is not a burden—it is a badge. Her entire life has been a celebration of Black excellence, southern pride, and ancestral strength. She has championed natural hair, darker tones, thick curves, and soulful expression in an industry that often ignored them.

Her message is rooted in unity: *We must build one another. Celebrate one another. And protect one another.* She challenges the community to pass on more than trauma—to pass on healing, entrepreneurship, legacy planning, and *love*.

She reminds us that being "the first" or "the only one" is not enough. We must *open the door wider*, and *teach those behind us how to walk through it without shrinking*.

To the World: Let Legacy Begin at Home

Finally, Tina's message to the world is a lesson in legacy-building. It starts not with fame or wealth—but with family. With character. With morning affirmations, Sunday dinners, shared dreams, and sacred values.

She reminds us that legacies are not built in boardrooms—they are built in *living rooms*. That greatness is not born under spotlights—it is forged in the hidden, holy places of everyday life.

And that every person, no matter where they begin, can create a legacy worthy of remembrance—if they live with courage, conviction, and care.

Acknowledgments

From Tina Knowles-Lawson (as imagined in memoir voice):

"To my mother, Agnéz Beyincé, thank you for the strength, the wisdom, and the unapologetic pride in our roots. You were my first teacher, my first stylist, and my eternal muse.

To Beyoncé and Solange, thank you for making me a mother with purpose. Watching you both become the powerful women you are today has been my greatest joy. You made me believe in legacy because you *became* it.

To Richard, my second chance at love—you are proof that healing is real, that joy can come in unexpected seasons, and that God always has more for us.

To the women in my life—sisters, cousins, clients, friends, stylists, and artists—thank you for walking this journey with me. You've each poured something sacred into my story.

To the Black community—you are my heart. Everything I've done has been to lift us higher, to show our worth, and to preserve our culture for generations to come.

To every dreamer holding a needle, a pen, a brush, a child, or a vision—*never let go of it*. This world needs what you carry.

And to every young girl who ever doubted her beauty, her brilliance, or her belonging—know this: You are more than enough. You are legacy in motion."

About the Author

C.J. Ellington is a dedicated researcher and gifted writer with a deep passion for telling powerful, purpose-driven stories. Specializing in biographical and memoir writing, Ellington has made it a personal mission to chronicle the lives of remarkable individuals—capturing their journeys with authenticity, elegance, and emotional depth.

With a background rooted in storytelling, social history, and cultural preservation, C.J. approaches every subject with reverence and curiosity, weaving together facts, feelings, and the fabric of legacy. Through extensive research and compelling narrative style, Ellington gives readers an intimate window into the lives of those who have shaped history, culture, and consciousness.

Matriarch: The Tina Knowles Memoir is one of many works in a growing collection that honors influential voices—particularly those whose stories empower, enlighten, and inspire generations.

When not writing, C.J. Ellington enjoys exploring archives, studying historical family lineages, and mentoring emerging biographers. Ellington believes that every life is a lesson—and every legacy deserves to be written.

Printed in Dunstable, United Kingdom